CONTENTS

INTRODUCTION

So, it's interesting to me what finally ended up being the "introduction" to this book, the introduction of me, my thoughts, experiences – my family, my world. In some respects, this was the most difficult part of the book to write.

I've re-written, edited, and outright deleted this section multiple times. I'm certain that the funniest, most clever, attention gripping version is somewhere on the cutting room floor as it were. I realized that attempts to be witty sounded less witty than I ever am, even accidentally, so I scrapped the idea altogether, and decided against a true introduction. With that admission, let me jump right into the pseudo introduction to save me the step of reformatting my Table of Contents.

You're undoubtedly reading this book for one of several reasons:

1) you're my wife
2) you're my kid
3) you're one of my best friends

Beyond those, odds are you either heard about this book from one of the 3 above, or the title simply caught your eye after searching Smashwords, Amazon, or iTunes with the keyword "parent."

In case you have no idea who I am, but you're fairly certain about the topic of this book with a title like "Confessions of a Horrible Parent," allow me to tell you a little bit about me, my wife, my kids, and why I decided to write this book.

My wife, Jamie, and I have been married for 25 years at the writing of this book. We live in a little 4A Texas town by the name of Argyle. We have 3 kids – now 20, 18, and 13. Our oldest, Chandler, always to be referred to as "my baby girl,"

is a Junior at the University of North Texas. Christian, is a Freshman at the University of Arkansas in gorgeous (and very cool) Fayetteville – go Razorbacks, or wooo pig sooie, or, ok, enough. Carson is an 8th grader at Argyle Middle School. (We also lost a 2 year old son, Corban, 15 years ago, but that's the subject of an entirely different book, although much of what has shaped my wife and I to become the parents we are today was birthed after his death. If you're interested in the details of that upcoming book, just message me on FB and you'll be one of the first to hear about it when I'm finished.)

If you're like me, you're skimming this prologue extremely quickly, eyes scanning for anything that flags "significant," in your mind, mostly desiring to hurry to what's deemed Chapter worthy, rather than throw-away, Intro fodder. I feel you. Of course, you want to get to the juicy stuff, I know, the horrible stuff. "Let's get to the confessions." Incidentally, if you're truly that type A, OCD bottom line, then jump immediately ahead to **Chapter 6.** Trust me, that'll scratch your "I like to watch a train wreck worse than mine to make myself feel a little better" itch! Haha

(quick caveat – if you're looking for Jerry Springer type horrible stuff – stuff that makes Chapter 6 look like a Disney movie, then you'll need to watch Jerry Springer – *is he still on?* Beating your 16 year old senseless, or dragging your out of control 4 year old daughter around by her hair, isn't parenting – it's abuse, and isn't the subject matter of this book – sorry to disappoint)

But if you're still with me here, I want to make a quick point that you'll hear reinforced throughout our time together. You're not as horrible a parent as you think you are. I know this isn't about you, but it really is, isn't it? We love confessions – as long as we're not the ones confessing. And I must confess, I'm good at confessing. I've made a regular habit of it, especially over the last 8 years of my life. I'll explain more on that later. For the simple fact that you purchased this book, I know you care deeply about your kids. You care what kind of parent you are, and how your kids "turn out," and that makes you ahead of the game automatically. Trust me on that. And although I'm going to let you know where I've blown it, screwed up, and terribly hurt my family, I want you also to hear the redemption and hope in my stories.

Because we care so deeply, means we are also our own worst critics, and means that we can be haunted by our failings when it comes to parenting. I'd say read with anticipation that not only will you connect and identify with the failings of me and my wife, but that you will find hope that you can 100%, positively, undoubtedly, walk away being a better parent, allowing the failures to lead you to being one of the best parents on the planet. Don't allow your mistakes in this, or any area for that matter, to define you. This isn't your ending. Let it be a beginning. Your story is still being written, and the pages are blank – *insert the 100 other cliché's here* – Don't waste the failures. Make them work for you, and for your kids. Make them matter.

If you could somehow magically just "know" my kids, then you might just begin taking notes on the next chapter. The Bible says, "you will know a tree by its fruit" and well, didn't Bill Cosby say, "the proof is in the pudding"? (or pudding pop, in the kitchen?) – sorry, may have mixed up that last one. Anyway, my kids are the bomb, and while it'd be the faux-humble thing to say at this point that it was all *in spite of* my wife and I, I actually know now that we actually *did* have a lot to do with how they "turned out" (good and bad, like it or not, so far, anyway).

And what about that? How in the world could any parent in their right mind dare write anything to do with parenting when their kids can still be claimed as dependents on their joint return? The audacity! And even if the kids are half way decent at this moment, you really want to take the risk of putting something in print when at any point, any of them could screw up royally, totally negating anything that's been written?

The point is, this isn't about raising perfect kids. Our kids have, and will, screw up. This isn't about being perfect, half-way perfect, or even great parents. Jamie and I have, and will, screw up. The fact is, there is no such thing as a perfect parent. As the Director of Pastoral Care at a large non-denominational church in Argyle, I've seen now over 400 couples or single parents, many of whom struggle with parenting issues of all kinds. You name it, I've heard it! And out of 400 couples or single parents, I still haven't met the parents who are doing everything right.

But what I have heard over the last 8 years, seeing between 20-30 parents a week, are some common themes. Themes in single-parent homes. Themes in blended family homes. Themes in low-income families. Themes in no income families. Themes in parenting post-divorce. Themes in parenting after the loss of a child or children to death. Themes in parents of special needs or autistic children. Themes in parenting kids with ADD and ADHD. Commonalities in parenting when one spouse is an addict, or when the parents are in a troubled marriage (again, due to a variety of factors – you name it, I've heard it – up close and personal!)

But here's the kicker. While my wife and I may only share certain things in common with many of the parents I just mentioned, in almost every meeting I have, I find myself at one point or another in the conversation saying, "me too." (There it is – I confess often, especially over the last 8 years, connecting with parents just like me.) People are people. Parents are parents. We have "common" issues, but the solutions are definitely NOT common sense. If they were, we'd all be parenting experts. We need to learn some *uncommon sense* thinking, concepts, tools, and methods if we want to become successful parents. We all love our kids and we do the best we can. We all make mistakes – some more than others. We all get it right sometimes, and we miss it sometimes.

What I've come to realize over the last 8 years of my parenting life, counseling people all day long, day in and day out, is that 100% of us have an opportunity to learn from our mistakes. In other words, no matter where you find yourself right now in your relationship with your kids, you have an opportunity to be a better parent. The fact that you're reading this book means that you're interested in being a better parent. You love your kids more than anyone will ever know, and you want some practical tips that will help you express that love more effectively, and that will deepen your relationships with your kids that will not only be rewarding now, but that will ensure that you "launch" incredible young adults into this crazy world, and that one day, you'll have a front row seat as a grandparent, witnessing the fruit of your labor as you watch your kids parent their kids in a loving, Godly way.

That's why Jamie and I want to be as transparent as possible, confessing how *horrible* we've been in our parenting journey thus far. It's because we've learned from our mistakes, and there has been healing in our confession. We are constantly learning. We want to do it right. We try. We try some more. We mess up – we try again. That doesn't work? Try something different. Oops, missed that one? That's okay, we'll get it next time.

And in the process, we are growing. We are gaining wisdom with every success and with every failure. We are wide awake, acutely aware of the importance of parenting well, intentionally, and on purpose. And I believe with that "wide awake" awareness, you, too, can be one of the best parents on the planet. I promise.

We invite you along with us on our messy, imperfect journey. In these pages, you will hear our voices, the voices of our own children, and the voices of the 400 couples that have taught me more than 100 doctoral degrees ever could.

Nice to meet you.

Chapter 1

Drop Your Baggage, Don't Hand It Off

~~~~~

"Pain that isn't transformed is transferred, and I fear I've transferred mine as well."
~~~~~

***Brennan Manning*[1]**

We have many names for it…junk, s@#$, stuff, baggage. We call it by many names, but no matter what we call it, we've all got it – the crap we bring into our marriages or relationships. (I'm gonna use crap – seems to be the safe word of choice by most folks my age talking about their stuff, I mean, crap.) What's interesting to me, in the hundreds of hours I spend talking with people about their crap, *most* don't even know where their crap came from. And if they *can* trace the origin, they still have absolutely no idea that it could be affecting them all these years later.

It's said that "time heals." I say to people all the time, "Time doesn't heal, it's just more time to be sick. Healing heals." So, while we always hear, "check your baggage at the door" when it comes to relationships, just how do we do that? Easier said than done, right? And what's the big deal, anyway? We all have our crap, so just deal with it. That's certainly a pervasive attitude in many people, but not a very helpful one. The *big deal* is that not only does our crap affect our spouse or relationship partner, but it also affects our kids. Most of what is transferred in parenting is *caught* not *taught*. We know the apple doesn't fall far from the tree, so if our kids are going to "come by it honestly" we want to make sure that "it" isn't full of crap – make sense?

I remember the time my daughter, Chandler, was about 9 or 10 years old. Overall, Chandler was an easy kid to raise - very compliant, wanted to please daddy, never got into the standard pre-teen drama that many of her peers thrived in. She wasn't openly defiant, and while definitely a confident, strong-willed child, she wasn't usually "sassy" when talking with her mother or me. That's why this particular instance stood out, I guess. Jamie had called her down for something, and Chandler shot back a look that would easily kill, and a sarcastic, disrespectful comment that immediately stopped me in my tracks. I sprung into action, and I flew around the corner before Jamie could even respond, and in retaliation (this was war), I shouted, "Don't you dare talk to your mother that way!" The instant the words escaped my lips, two things happened simultaneously. One, Chan gave me the most incredulous, "how could YOU of all people?..." kind of look, and two, a voice whispered in my ear, "you taught her that."

Now, before unpacking that story a bit more, I want to take a minute to talk about that voice. I've come to recognize that seemingly *inner* voice as the voice of God. Some, like me, might call this the voice of God. Some might call it the Holy Spirit, Jesus, a higher power, the universe, or a number of other names for God in other cultures or religious contexts. For me, what's interesting is that it's not an "outer" voice, rather more like someone inside me that sounds a lot like me, arresting me in the moment, teaching me something I need to know about myself. There's an instant heightened sense of self-awareness, coupled with an unusual humility to actually realize that what the voice is saying is correct, and that it demands immediate attention. (I haven't always heard that voice, and for a time, when that voice did speak, I wouldn't be so quick to listen, rather would usually defensively dismiss it.) Now I trust it, and try not to ignore it. Enough about the voice.

Bursting into tears, my daughter ran into the other room and threw herself face down into the couch, smothering her face with a pillow. I went in and sat down on the couch next to her, and began to rub her hair. After an initial flinch, she allowed my hand to continue, and then I quietly said, "Sweetheart, I'm sorry. Daddy taught you that." Chandler then peeked up at me with the one eye that wasn't stuffed into the pillow. I continued, "I know I've talked to your mom that way, and you learned it from me. I want you to know I'm sorry I've modeled that, and it's not right. It's not right for me, and it's not right for you. You forgive me, and I'll forgive you, but we both need to stop doing that, and start treating your mom with respect."

That was a defining moment in my marriage. It was also a defining moment in my relationship with my daughter. I believe Chandler learned several things during that interaction. One, parents aren't perfect, and they mess up. Two, that "daddy was willing to own his mistakes and say I'm sorry, so maybe I can too". I also believe Chandler gained respect for me that day, and also walked away knowing that I loved her and that she was a good kid, rather than feeling like a screw up, wondering if daddy loved her. (Who knows, she might have even wondered what could have changed my attitude so quickly after jumping on her – we eventually had the talk about "the voice" that had arrested me that day.)

Even deeper than what makes us angry in the moment, is coming to understand where our anger comes from in the first place. This is such a common piece of baggage, I feel the need to touch on it. You see, long before Chandler was born, I was blowing up, throwing temper tantrums, going into fits of rage on a semi-regular basis. This wasn't the case with me growing up, or prior to being married, so naturally, I blamed it on my wife. The truth is, I was responsible for my anger, not her, and after almost losing my marriage, I went on a quest to figure out why I was so angry.

This is a complex subject, because there are such a huge variety of things that make us angry, so I'll just focus on one example. Psychology would tell us that underlying anger is fear (hard thing for tough guys to admit). Even if we do buy that, where does our fear come from, and what are we afraid of? In his book, Wild At Heart, John Eldredge, a leading expert on "father wounds," says that masculinity is bestowed on young men by other men.[2] So, boys growing up without fathers – fathers who have left, fathers who are present, but emotionally absent, work-a-holic, distant fathers, etc. – have a huge question mark hanging over their heads. "Do I have what it takes?" And that question takes many forms as we go through life – Will I be able to come through? How do I become a father? What does a good husband do? Can I land a job? Can I keep a job? Will I be able to be a good provider? Will I be able to relate to a teen-age daughter, a teen-age son? And the list goes on and on.

And for many men, because their father didn't answer those questions for them, the insecurity they feel brings fear, resulting in their walking around clueless, but afraid to admit it, leading to anger. Wives say, "he's just angry at the world" and she has no idea why. (side note – so if men don't allow God to answer their questions for them, they look to the wrong sources for their answer – extra-marital affairs, porn, work, sports, even their wives – and none of these can answer the questions for them, leading to more frustration and anger, withdrawal, escape, addiction – medication of their pain in a variety of ways) These men allow their anger and rage to plague them, taking it out on their kids for seemingly no reason. Sound familiar?

I recall a scene that happened one summer day while the boys and I were out back swimming. Carson was only about 8 at the time, which would have put Christian around 13. While I'll admit our pool games got pretty wild, and possibly bordered on extremely dangerous, this particular moment had gotten way out of hand, and I had called for a truce, waving the white flag. Imagine this, Christian wouldn't stop. Hmm, that'd be weird. Whatever it was that he was doing, (can't remember details, but I do remember something about Carson drowning!) he wouldn't let up, and Carson's screaming turned to crying, and wild flailing before I finally stepped in to stop the torture and force the boys back to their corners. What started to really bother me wasn't Carson's tears – I knew he'd live – rather it was Christian's cavalier attitude and smirking as he kept throwing verbal jabs at Carson, taunting him for being a "baby." This really got under my skin, and I sat Christian down, and started in on him. I mean I really let him have it, which might seem justified, but this was overboard. Something was touched deep inside of me, and set me off, and my anger, and volume was escalating, and I went into a tirade that was not to be curbed, even with Christian's now humble posture as he diverted his eyes to the ground, and began to scowl. Christian knew the punishment didn't fit the crime, and that somehow he was paying for the sins of someone else in my past. He didn't know why the volcano was there in the first place, but he knew the eruption was happening and that the hot lava was being spewed all over him. One phrase in particular stands out as I think back on that day. It was me saying, rather yelling, "Son, you don't know when to stop! You just keep on keeping on, dogging him until he's pissed, or hurt." More on my anger later, but suffice it to say that I was doing exactly to Christian what I was lambasting him for doing to his brother.

What about women who never had fathers? Who were abused? Who were molested? Where do feelings of abandonment, rejection, and worthlessness go if not healed? How do they play out in a life, in a marriage, in a mom? Obviously, there is so much more, and so many lies we believe about ourselves because of our families of origin, our past relationships and ex-spouses. We've even allowed coaches, teachers, and friends to tell us who we are (and who we're not). Most of us hear those voices on a daily basis – especially when we lie down at night, or wake up in the morning. It's funny how those tapes play and will haunt us if not healed. And again, pain that's not healed is transferred, so we have moms who are flying off the handle at the drop of a hat, instilling fear in their children, rather than nurturing love, affection, and confidence.

Recently, my family took a vacation to Gulf Shores, Alabama. One morning, my 13 year old son, Carson, and I were down at the beach making a sand man (carving a figure of a dude lying on his back in the sand). I had gone out snorkeling for a bit, and when I got back, my son had an embarrassed look on his face, and was fish-eyeing an altercation between a mother and her son (about the same age as Carson). She was ripping him a new one, and in an extremely loud voice, shaming him in front of everyone around. As she finally made a gesture with her hand (backhanding the air a few feet from his face – as if to say, "I'm done with you!") she stormed away and began rehashing the episode with her lady friends. My son began re-telling me everything he had seen and heard. What's interesting is that even Carson knew who was truly in the wrong in this situation. And if he felt a bit of that boy's shame as the mother lit into him, what did that boy feel? What kind of lasting effect will that have on that boy as he grows into adult-hood? Will he file that away somewhere and pull it out one day while he disciplines his son at the beach?

But here's what you might find more interesting. Rather than wondering what that boy did to deserve that *or not,* or passing judgment on that irate mom, my first thought was, "man, I wonder how she was wounded by her mom or dad." And even if I don't always go there, at the very least, I always wonder why the perpetrator in that crime is hurting. Hurt people hurt people. You may find this odd that I think of these kinds of things when I see these types of behaviors, but remember, it's not just me rubber-necking at the scene of a train wreck, it's that little voice that does it to me as well.

What about the deeper, more troubling issues? I've talked about the impact on a child from an absentee father – but how about one who *is* there, but who constantly criticized or berated their child? Or physically or sexually abused a child? Children of alcoholic parents? Children of drug addicted parents? The list could go on, but we'll leave it at this – you get the point. Although it goes without saying, I'm not saying here, don't be an alcoholic or abusive parent. I'm saying that if you were a victim of those things growing up, chances are you've got baggage – crap that desperately needs to be healed so that you don't pass it along to the next generation. Your kids will pass it to their kids. Crap rolls downhill! You need to stop it with you. (In the Appendix, I'll mention some good resources for healing wounds in these areas.)

Chapter 2

Catch Them Doing Something Right

~~~~~

"And a voice came from heaven: 'You are my Son, whom I love; with you I am well pleased'.'"
~~~~~

Let's have a little pop quiz. For those of you who just broke out into a sweat, there will be no grades, and there are no wrong answers. (Didn't you love when teachers would say this after asking a question? You knew it was a lie!) Here's the question: To which do you respond more positively in your life, praise or criticism? If you said criticism, please email me right away and get in for a session. For most of us, this is a no brainer. Praise vs. Criticism – Praise wins! Every time.

But let's face it, it's easier to find something your kid is doing wrong than it is to "catch them doing something right" – mainly because they do more wrong that right, right? (correct?) I mean, by definition, kids are kids, and well, aren't kids *supposed* to screw up? Recently, I was talking with a mother and father of several young kids, all under 10, and was giving them this line, and the mom quickly retorted, "that'd be great if he ever did anything right!" (me: "haha" *nervous laughter* – really thinking, "poor kid.")

Okay, so I know they're young kids and can really be a pain in the butt sometimes, but, I think that's going to be my point here. They ARE KIDS! Yes, we want to raise them, discipline them, correct them, teach them, but they are KIDS! We want them to become mature, but they are still immature. We want them to become responsible, but they are irresponsible. Oh, did I mention THEY'RE KIDS!?

So, perhaps we need to take a quick self-inventory and ask ourselves when is the last time we caught our kids doing something right. I'm sure we won't have to think back too far to remember the last time we corrected our kids or pointed out something they did wrong. But what about catching them doing something right? What would that look like? Better yet, what would that sound like?

Before I answer that question, let me tell you what it doesn't sound like, and illustrate why this is so important in the first place.

I mentioned that anger was my nemesis in the early years, and that some of it stemmed from some family of origin stuff, and previous wounds left unhealed. One of the nice little pieces of luggage I brought into adulthood was that pesky little disease called perfectionism. (Some delusional people actually wear "perfectionist" as a badge of honor – poor souls) Yes, I was/am a perfectionist – desperately *needing* things in my world to be perfect

– especially things that I did/do. It wasn't so much that I *wanted* things to be perfect, like some control freaks. I needed them to be perfect because what I did was a direct reflection of me. Somehow, I learned that my performance was going to be judged, praised or criticized, by anyone and everyone, who were all most definitely scrutinizing me, and were ready to pounce on the slightest flaw or mistake, relegating me to the stupid idiot that I truly was.

Where did I learn this? Certainly people can be judgmental, and sometimes our nature is to laugh at others' mistakes. Human nature can be mean like that when not brought into check by a higher power. But, come on, was EVERYONE always watching me? Could they actually have cared less what I did or whether or not I made a mistake? Where in the world was I taught that people were critical, and that in order to avoid scathing reviews, one had to be perfect? Unfortunately, I believe I learned it in my family growing up. For the sake of brevity, I won't dissect this to the core, but suffice it to say that this disease was pervasive in my family, and yes, we "came by it honestly." Remember, CRD! (CRD – This is the convenient acronym I'll throw out from now on when deemed necessary, rather than writing crap rolls downhill").

I'll just give a quick illustration of what I'm talking about. A couple of years ago (so, I would have been in my mid 40s), I attended a weekend experience at Gateway Church in Southlake, TX called *Kairos*. For those of you Greek scholars out there that know what this word means, congratulations. For the other 99.9% of us, let me give you the definition. Kairos is pregnant time, the time of possibility – moments in our day, our week, our month, our year or our lifetime that define us. It is a crossroads. It has the ripe opportunity to make you bitter or better. It is a teachable moment.

Man, I love this. I mean I just love the definition. That's a cool definition. That's what I love about Greek words – there is so much packed in one word. Plus, it just sounds cool – Kairos. (and it makes me think of that syrup my mom used to mix in with peanut butter to make the smoothest PB sandwiches ever! Yum!) But I digress.

So, for the pastors at Gateway Church who organize Kairos, their prayer is that it would be *the* right or opportune moment for you. And was it ever for me! Following one of the teachings about how God wants to speak to us about lies we've believed about ourselves that might have kept us bound in our lives, we were instructed to simply ask God to reveal those lies, and then tell us the truth. Sounded easy enough. Just the instruction alone made me realize how rarely I got that specific when questioning God about things.

So, there I went – "God, are there any lies that I believe about myself, and when did I begin believing that lie?" BOOM!! No, I didn't hear a boom. I didn't hear a sound. But it was that quick – boom! The answer wasn't in the form of a sound or words. Immediately, I was transported back to a scene I hadn't thought about in years. Remember I told you I was around 45 at the time. The scene that God had teleported me back to in my mind happened when I was in 3rd grade. I was in my childhood home, standing in the doorway of the spare bedroom, which doubled as my dad's "office," remembering the conversation that would define me for years to come.

Earlier that night, I had been in a play at my elementary school. I was often picked to be the lead role in plays or musicals, being a bit of a big fish in a small pond. I loved the feeling I got when I "performed" well in those plays, recitals, or talent shows. I could see the pride in my parents, their approving smiles and laughter as we snapped pics – I basked in the afterglow. We all did. Not so this night.

That infamous night, when my time to shine came, I froze! I stood there on that stage, mouth half open, totally choking – forgetting the words I knew by heart, and could have recited in my sleep. They just wouldn't come. I don't remember much about the rest of the show. I literally couldn't tell you which show it even was. But it is interesting what I do recall. I remember there were no photo opps after this particular program. I remember my parents walking uncharacteristically quickly to the car that night, well in front of me.

So, back to the Kairos-induced scene. I can't remember now why I would have gone into my dad's office that night – maybe to see if he was on the phone, perhaps sensing the inevitable, wanting to get it over with. But there I stood, and the scene played in my mind so vividly, you'd never know that it had been 36 years since it actually happened. My dad looked up at me from his computer, spun toward me in his chair, and with that look where his eyebrows scrunched together and the corners of his lips curled up, he said, "Son, when you forget your lines, don't just stand there looking like a *dummard*, look up over the audience and stare at the back until you can remember your lines."

Now, I'm not sure I had heard that word before, and I'm positive I haven't heard anyone use it since, but something told me in my 3rd grade brain that "dummard" was some derivative of dumb. But there it was. God had exposed a moment (if not THE moment) when I began to believe that in order to receive love, I had to perform perfectly. Mistakes weren't tolerated. They were embarrassing. I was embarrassing. Forgetting lines was shameful. I was ashamed. I made my parents ashamed when I messed up. I looked like a dummard when I messed up (you can't see this, but a red line just popped up under dummard – there it goes again – see, even my Macbook Pro doesn't know what a dummard is)

As God began to unpack scene after scene in what seemed like my life flashing before my eyes, I began to weep. At first, I began to feel self-conscious (for all I know I was beginning to look like a dummard – haha – sorry I couldn't resist). That is, until I noticed most everyone around me doing the same thing. I knew lies were being exposed all around the room that day. God began to tell me the truth. That it was actually ok to mess up, to not be perfect. That most people aren't that critical and don't even notice half of the mistakes that we worry about. He let me know that people would still love me, maybe even more, if I weren't perfect.

The healing that day was phenomenal, and the freedom I've experienced since has been nothing short of a miracle. And it's changed every interaction I have with my children. I realize now that something I say to my 13 year old, Carson, could stay with him, haunting him into his 40s, 50s, heck, until he goes to Kairos!

So, after a band concert when he misses a note or two? – "Hey, great job tonight, sonny. Did you have fun?" "What? No, I hardly noticed. That's no big deal." "Oh, I'm sorry you felt embarrassed – man, I'm so proud of you, you could have picked your nose up there, and I would have been cheering." (yes, I've said that – usually gets a laugh. If not, I go into the dummard story)

After a not-so-hot performance on the football field? – "Hey, great game bud. Way to work hard. I'm so proud of you. You have fun?" "That's cool. Yeah, I had some games like that. You'll come back strong next week." "Did you hear mom cheering for you out there, man she nearly broke my ear drums?"

Missed a few spots mowing the yard? – "Hey bud, great job on the yard. I appreciate you doing that." (when they're 10, and just learning, you leave it at that, and go clean up after them, hitting all the spots they missed) If they're still missing spots at 13? "Hey bud, great job on the yard. I really appreciate you doing that. Go ahead and grab your shoes, and come on out here with me, I want to show you a couple of things…"

You get the idea? You praise them over and over again. Do it as often as you can. Do you ever get tired of hearing praise? Find something to be proud of, and be specific. The more specific the praise, the better. I once heard a teen-aged girl tell her mom, "You always said you were proud of me, and it never meant anything, because you never told me what you were proud of." And although that's always stuck with me, I'll bet you dollars to donuts she still felt loved every time her mom said it.

Some of you might be saying to yourself, "Yeah, but isn't there a time for constructive criticism? I mean, it's not all gum-drops and roses out there in the real world. You don't want to set them up for failure, making them think everything they do is great. They'll be in for a rude awakening…"

Is there a time for correction, for discipline, for training? Absolutely. Do it with praise. Constructive criticism? You tell me – does criticism generally build you up, or tear you down? Is it constructive or destructive? I'd say be very careful when it comes to correcting your children, no matter what age. Maybe just drop the criticism part and go for constructive. We're all about building up in the Hackney home – there's plenty of criticism out there in the "real world." We want to create an environment where our kids know they're loved, no matter what – no matter how they play, perform, look – they know they are ok.

And for the record, when kids that are raised in this kind of environment encounter that "rude" awakening in the real world, they actually recognize that critical spirit as just that, rude behavior, and actually tend not to believe a word of it. This is because the two people that God gave the power to speak truth into their lives told them that they were ok, and the kids believe it.

A couple of quick Post Scripts to this chapter:

1. Wanted you to know that I have totally made peace with my father, and the whole dummard thing. I know he was only trying to help me do better next time, and had nothing but my best interests at heart. (Most likely, his dad called him dummard on occasion – who knows? – haven't circled back to that one just yet.) Point is, I've forgiven him for this, and he

probably never thought twice about it.

2. I cannot emphasize enough the POWER that fathers possess to speak blessing over their children, literally shaping the course of their lives for the good. Downside is, along with this HUGE power to bless, also comes the power to curse. The power for such strong positive wouldn't be real without the potential for the negative. Power is power, and it is real, dads! Use it for good! You are speaking life or death over your kid at any given moment. You are shaping them in some way – building them up, or tearing them down. Now, I'm not saying that moms aren't important, or that their voice doesn't carry significant weight. They are absolutely essential for nurturing, guiding, caring, loving, etc. It's just that DAD has been given extra special power by God – he sets the tone, for good or bad, in the home. Take this one to the bank. For those of you single moms reading this, more about this dilemma later.

Chapter 3
Make Your Default Answer "Yes"

~~~~~

"I imagine that yes is the only living thing."

E.E. Cummings[4]

I'll make this chapter short and sweet. (thank me later)

If I had a nickel for every time a family comes to me about their "out of control" teen-ager, I'd be a rich man (well, at least I wouldn't be driving a Hyundai Elantra – no offense, Hyundai)

As I dive into the family dynamics in these situations, I'm almost always sure to find an over-bearing, controlling parent who is demanding that a kid "fall in line", do as they say, and whenever even slightly questioned as to "why?" – it's always a terse "BECAUSE I SAID SO!"

What I've found to be true, (this shouldn't actually be a surprise as it comes to most of us intuitively) is that *control* begets *rebellion*. (Can you use beget
~~~~~

when not giving a genealogy?, Oh well, I said it – beget. Beget, beget, beget – the other day, my 13 year old said, "dad, have you ever noticed when you say a word over and over and over, after a while, it doesn't sound like a word anymore?" Haha – but now I'm way off base – where were we?) When someone feels controlled, they naturally rebel. Conversely, when people feel free, and unhindered, they tend not to rebel. What's there to rebel against? You'd think that more parents would understand this core principle, and allow it to guide their parenting and discipline practices, but many don't.

It's easy to understand why, though – I mean why parents feel the need to control their kids. The conversation goes like this:

> "I'm the parent, they're the child and no kid of mine is going to rule the roost."
>
> "I never questioned MY parents – If I would have, I would have been back-handed into next week."
>
> "I've lived longer than they have, and I know best."
>
> "I just want them to avoid the mistakes that I've made."
>
> "I'm just worried that they're going to make a colossal mistake that's going to cost them big time consequences."

We've all heard these, and more. Heck, we've all said most, if not all of these at one time or another. We heard these things from our parents, and many of us heard more than our share of "because I said so's" growing up. So, control was a) modeled, and then b) control comes a bit naturally as a result of love and concern mixed with a little wisdom and fear. Maybe it's not all bad, then. I mean, it is our job to raise our children, to train them, to teach them, to correct them, to discipline them, right?

And because we so desperately want to protect them from making life-altering mistakes, many times our default answer is "no." (or NO or even H#$% NO!) Recently, while attending the AACC Conference in Nashville, TN, the comedian Tim Hawkins (hilarious, by the way) did a funny bit about parents trying to be "cool" so their kids will like them. I won't do Tim the injustice of trying to re-tell his jokes, but his basic point was that he couldn't care less whether or not his teenager liked him or thought he was cool. He quipped, "I'm not your friend or your buddy, I'm your parent." He went on to demonstrate, in a hysterical variety of voices, songs, and gestures, all the creative ways he says NO to his kids. And while he does hit the bulls-eye on our kid dominated, soft-parenting culture, many have chosen the extreme opposite, deciding to clamp down and never allow their kid to do anything they ask. A mom told me one time, "I usually don't even listen anymore, I just immediately say no, then if she starts to argue, I'll come up with reasons why not." Obviously, this parent rules the roost in her home, but I wonder if she's getting the respect and trust that she desires from her daughter?

So, when does good discipline cross the line into controlling behavior that has negative lasting effects on children? I don't know – you tell me. Why don't we start by seeing if our child is always frustrated, angry, acting out, or rebellious? In other words, rather than me telling you what constitutes damaging controlling behavior, why don't you tell me if your kid feels like they're being controlled. Some might say, "don't they all – especially teenagers?"

Actually, no, they don't. Recently, I asked my 20 year old daughter, Chandler, if she felt controlled as a teenager, and why or why not. The following is a quote:

"No, I didn't feel controlled as a teenager. You guys let me do what I wanted, and I felt like I had freedom to make my own choices as long as I didn't make any bad ones or give you any reason to step in. People might think that 'letting me do what I wanted' has a negative connotation because of kids getting into drugs, or alcohol, but that's not what I wanted to do."

So, what's the secret? Why did Chandler, and now Christian and Carson, feel so much freedom, and *for the most part*, do what we wanted them to do, making wise choices when it came to activities, behaviors, and friends? I believe it's because we made our default answer "yes." We made a decision early on that we wanted to show our kids that we trusted them, and that we believed they had the maturity to make good choices and wise decisions, even at an early age. So, we said yes a lot. "Dad, can I go to the movies with Ashley and Madison?" "Sure, sweetie." "Dad, can I go to the mall with Amanda, then sleep over at her house tonight?" "Sure, baby, that sounds good." I explained to our kids that as long as they did what they said they were going to do, and were actually where they said they were going to be, with the people they said they were going to be with, then they'd get a lot of yes's. In other words, I trust you until you give me a reason not to. As long as you don't break my trust, I'm going to respect your requests.

Now, respecting requests with a fair consideration doesn't actually mean that *every* request is going to get a yes. Jamie and I have, and will, continue to say no plenty of times. But here's the beauty in making your default answer yes. When the kids see that you honor their "asks," and are usually met with a yes, they react a lot better to the "No's" when they come. If they are met with constant no's, frustration builds in them, and they huff, argue, and tend to pout, get angry, and act out in any number of negative ways. (Side note, get over your pride, and actually explain your No's a little further than "because I said so." Most kids respond better to an explanation than the prideful remark demanding respect)

Asking yourself why you do the things you do is a good discipline to learn, and one that I believe is helpful in any situation. Applied to saying no, it can help you discern which No's are valid, and which ones you might want to rethink.

"Did I just say no because I'm in a bad mood?"

"Did I just say no because I'm tired and don't want to mess with giving him a ride?"

"Did I just say no because I'm being lazy and don't want to do the leg work to research who she's going to spend the night with?"

"Did I just say no because his dad said yes?" – haha (not funny)

I remember being surprised one day, when Christian was a senior in HS, and he had texted me, "Can I go to (his girlfriend at the time) house?" When I saw the text, I had just heard the weather report, saying freezing rain and sleet was going to blanket the metroplex for the next several days. What's funny, out of habit, I almost just said "sure." (I had literally said yes the previous 10-15 times he had asked to spend time with her or his friends.) Instead of texting back, I picked up the phone, and explained to Christian about the weather, and that I wanted him to stay in that night. Are you ready for this? He said, "Ok." That's it. OK. And you didn't hear his tone of voice obviously, but I did. No huff, no disappointment. Again, I was surprised at the quick and easy, unforced, light-hearted "ok" that he offered.

My next thought? "What a good kid." Made me wish for clearing weather so I could say yes again soon.

I'm telling you, it works.

Try it! Today! (I know, I know, somebody just said under their breath – "No")

Chapter 4

Tell Them Who They Are, Not Who They're Not

~~~~~

"To be or not to be- that is the question"

Hamlet[5]

I can remember it like it was yesterday. I was still in college at Abilene Christian University, but had gone to visit mom and dad, who were living in Rochester, NY at the time. My mom and I had just gone to a corner grocery store, and we were sitting in the parking lot about to leave. She was bragging on something (what, I can't recall), but after she went on and on for several minutes, I jumped in and said, "Mom, I appreciate all that, but that's not about me, that's about God in me." Striking some nerve, (to this day, I haven't figured out how or why), she turned to me and with a bit of a scowl said, "You're flawed!"

Ok. Yes ma'am. Got it. Flawed. So, I don't remember how the conversation went the rest of the way home. I think I probably stared out the window trying to figure out what had just happened, but one word stuck with me for years. It could be recalled at the drop of a hat, especially if anyone threw a disapproving look my way, or made me feel less than perfect in any given situation. Flawed. I'm flawed. Am I flawed? Isn't everyone? (Sometimes I'd recite Romans 3:23 in the Bible to myself so as not to feel too badly for myself)

Whatever point my mom was trying to make in that situation – whatever teaching she might have been trying to do, failed to hit the mark. Rather than understanding any sort of positive principle my mom wanted me to grasp in that Piggly Wiggly parking lot, I simply walked away knowing she felt that I was in fact, flawed. (Flawed makes a nice companion to dummard. Can one be a flawed dummard? I think one can.)

So, think of the names you've been called in your life. Some of you already did – just as you were reading my story, your own story played in your head. You heard that name again – stupid, liar, lazy, dishonest, dummard…Wait, no? Not dummard? – crap, I knew I was the only one.

Bless our parents' hearts – they meant well. Again, they loved us, and were
~~~~~

just trying to teach us not to be those things they just called us. Anyway, I'm just glad we learned from their mistakes, and we would never call our kids any of those things. Whew! (for those of you who might have missed that – yes, sarcasm)

Alright, you know where I'm going with this now.

What if we were to reframe the stories for our kids' future replay?

Let's say we catch one of our kids lying to us. How about we remind them of the importance of telling the truth, becoming trustworthy, and tell them that Hackney's are truth tellers. "We tell the truth in this family, we don't lie." "Come on son, you know you're not a liar, you're honest – what got into you?" "That's not like you, that's not who you are!"

And you can begin to come up with your own script. Write it – rehearse it ahead of time, so that you don't revert back to the default – the tapes that you could so easily pull out from your own stories. Here are a few more samples:

"Come on son, that's not your best work – I've seen your best. Don't settle for that, I know you're not lazy, give it another shot. Give it your best." You're a hard worker when you want to be."

"Come on, man, you're smarter than that. Don't be stupid" (So, I threw in this example to show you, you can still use the word stupid. It actually comes in real handy when dealing with teenage boys) Just don't call them stupid. Tell them not to *act* stupid. But the key is to *lead* with "you're smarter than that." Tell them who they are – smart, not who they're not – stupid!

"Sweetheart, you're more responsible than that." That's not like you at all.

"Hey, use your good judgment – you know better than that."

Reframing your words in little ways, can make a big difference, now, and believe it or not, for years to come. Your kid walks away believing in themselves. They do this because they hear what you believe about them. It's subtle, but it's huge:

"I'm a hard worker, I'm smart, I'm responsible, and I've got good judgment."

Sounds a lot better than lazy, dumb, irresponsible, lying fool doesn't it?

Sixteen year-old boys are just hard! You all feel me. I mean girls aren't a cake walk -(ours happened to be, but most of you have the middle school drama that might even carry over into, well, now) But, in general, most of us admit that girls are a little easier to raise. Boys are difficult. They get that driver's license, and go brain dead. They don't mean to, bless their little, red-blooded American boy, pea-picking hearts! It's really not their fault. They have car keys, an ever increasing sense of independence establishment, and enough hormones to power an electricity grid for the state of Texas. Somewhere in there, their brains fall out.

I've seen dozens of families, and dozens of 16-17 year old boys, encountering similar challenges during this season of the boys' lives. As I hear story after story of boys' slipping grades, ignored curfews, and all around disrespectful behavior, I have to admit that I've felt some comfort personally knowing we're not alone, and that my kid is normal. The very fact that I can relate, and can look other parents in the eye and say, "your boy is normal – that's just part of being 17," seems to grant parents permission to let out a collective sigh of relief. "So we're not horrible parents?" they always ask. I quickly say, "Well, I didn't say THAT, you might be." Haha – seriously though, they really might be psycho parents. I'm teasing! (Cuckoo)

Raising a 16 year old boy/young man/man wannabe is enough to make you feel crazy for sure. I still remember when Christian turned 16. Up to that point, he had been no problem. Great kid, tons of respect, well mannered, good grades, no drama. Heck, I taught him to drive, so I was fairly excited about him being able to take himself and his brother to school, and that he would soon be working, contributing to car, insurance, gas, and Whataburger expenses.

One morning, Carson came to me and said, "Dad, why did Christian come in at 4:30 this morning?" Carson had slept on the couch the night before. (Carson never really started sleeping in a bed until about middle school – he liked to sleep at numerous locations around the house until about the age of 12 – that was cool with us – weird, but cool – he's our creative kid!)

I said, "Carson, that is a GREAT QUESTION! I'll make sure and get back with you on that right after I murder your brother." After employing methods somewhere between time out and waterboarding, Christian eventually confessed to "sneaking out" the night before. Sneaking out!? SNEAKING OUT??? That's stuff that stupid kids did. Christian didn't SNEAK OUT, I assured myself. But he had. He did! I was in a bit of shock that MY SON had finally done something that those *other kids* did – you know those juvenile delinquent types.

Once I reminded myself that we weren't in fact, *special*, or different, or immune to brain-dead 16 yr old boys, I proceeded to ask Christian to come upstairs so we could have a chat. Privacy in these cases is a good call. Could the younger siblings learn a thing or two by listening in to "the chat" about such issues? Absolutely. But some talks are best in private between a parent and the perpetrator. The goal is to avoid shaming the kid in front of other family members. (Sometimes, what Carson imagines is probably worse than the actual "lecture," so it's still an effective tool with him, even when he's not privy to the conversation)

So, what followed was a great talk about why Christian felt the need to sneak out in the first place. He actually shared at a deep emotional level his fear of being made fun of ("ripped a new one") by his older sister if he were to ask about going out late at night. So, to avoid embarrassment, he just decided he'd sneak out. So, together, we established the undeniable fact that his first impulse in how to solve that problem was a bad idea. Then, we talked through how much the family loved him, and any good-natured ribbing was just that, especially when he asked if he could leave to go see his girlfriend at 11:45 p.m. – another bad idea. We talked about leaving earlier in the evening so he could be in at a decent hour, respecting our curfew for him, and respecting his girlfriend's father's wishes.

Throughout the talk, I reminded Christian that he was a good kid, and that I so appreciated all the ways he had shown us respect through the years, and that this just wasn't like him. I told him what I truly believed about him, his heart, and the way he should act to live up to who I believed he was. To my knowledge, Christian never snuck out again. (key words – "to my knowledge") No, seriously, key words – "I told him what I truly believed about him."

Another time, after Christian had missed his curfew for a third time in a row (there would be more…), we were again upstairs, with him sitting on my bed, me in the little chair that never gets used unless I'm scooting it up for "a chat". I was laying into him, asking him how in the heck he could just blow off another curfew, especially after repeated offenses, and given the amount of grace we had bestowed upon him to date. His flippant attitude just wasn't ok. Just minutes earlier downstairs, when asked "what about 10:30 do you not understand, and why weren't you home by 10:30?," he had shrugged his shoulders and made that little slight frown with a snort and bulging eyes (his best incredulous impersonation, done when a parent is definitely over-reacting), and said with a smirk, "because I wasn't."

Wrong answer.

He would later regret having said that.

Ironically, earlier that night, I had been reading Brennan Manning's book, All is Grace, and I was in the chapter where he says the quote I mentioned at the top of Chapter 1, "pain that isn't healed is transferred, and I fear I've transferred mine as well." That quote haunts me, but it also helps me. While I constantly beat myself up for making mistakes, and for teaching my kids my crap (CRD), I'm also acutely aware of things that need to change, things that need to stop with me – so as not to transfer my anger (for one) to my kids. So, all that was stirred up in a nice, little, raw, exposed nerve, as my fist came crashing down on the island in the kitchen, bursting into a fit of rage, forcing Christian upstairs.

Several things happen during these explosions. Some of you undoubtedly identify with me here. You immediately hate yourself for your out of control burst of rage. "There you go again, blowing it, doing exactly what you just vowed you'd never do again", feeling convicted by the latest story you're reading, or worse yet, the recent encounter that left your kid fearing you, rather than respecting you. So, now you're dealing with your own feelings of guilt, mixed with feelings of anger toward your disrespectful kid. You know you need to discipline your child, but you fear wounding your child, doing damage to them that will cause them to hate you forever, and inevitably set their course of spending hundreds of dollars in therapy in their thirties.

This story reinforces the importance of chapter 1, dropping our baggage so we don't hand it off, but it also demonstrates how hard it is to parent well. This isn't common sense stuff, and it's also not for the weak, or the faint of heart. After this type of explosion (the one that happened downstairs), many parents fold. They silence the kid, shut them down, punish them, and go medicate themselves with a few beers or a bottle of wine – the entire bottle. It's easy to retreat from the battle here.

You can't retreat. You HAVE TO ENGAGE. Get back in the game. Do not forfeit. Right now is when your kid needs to hear who they are more than ever. "Does dad hate me?" "Does mom think I'm a horrible kid?" "Will they ever love me again?"

This is when you have to go *upstairs*, assume the position, and finish well. First, take your lumps and admit your own mistakes. Admit that you blew it in anger, and that your outburst wasn't appropriate. Own that. I can still remember when Christian, in his natural defensive posture, said, "Dad, you're being an ass-hole."

Wow, I thought. He just said that. We don't say that in this house. You can't speak to me that way was what I was thinking. What I was actually thinking was, "My son now sneaks out, and calls me an ass-hole. I am a parenting GURU!"

I can't say this, or any other isolated incident always ended where Christian felt amazing, and I felt like a Pulitzer Prize winning dad. What I can say is through a series of engaged, intentional moments, where Jamie and I refused to retreat, Christian was reminded over and over again who he was, what we believed about him, and how much we loved him.

The culmination of all of these moments made a memory that will last as long as I live. Christian again sat at the foot of my bed, after blowing it about as badly as a HS kid can blow it. After being "busted," he sat with his head hung in shame, crying, repeating, "I'm sorry, I'm so sorry, I know I was wrong. I don't know what I was thinking."

Because of his brokenness, and lack of defiance, and the fact that he was showing true remorse, the true heart of his father was exposed and displayed. (Similar to the heart of our Father, the one that is the author of "the voice" in Chapter 1)

I leaned forward in my chair, I put my hands under his chin, lifted his face to mine, looked him in the eyes and said, "Son, it's ok. I love you, son. Do you hear me? I've never been more proud of you." What was said between the two of us will remain between just the two of us, but it was beautiful. Christian heard his father whisper again to his heart who he truly was, not who he was not.

To this day, it was one of the hardest, and best days of my parenting life.

Chapter 5

Parent on the Same Page

~~~~~

"…Every kingdom divided against itself will be ruined, and every city or household divided against itself will not stand."

Jesus[6]

As I start this chapter, I realize that many of you reading this are single parents, or parents in a blended family situation. I've actually had you in mind every day I write, but this chapter specifically talks about being "on the same page" with your spouse, obviously creating a bit of a challenge for those of you not living with a spouse or the other biological parent of your child. I will come back and address a few of the most common issues I see when dealing with blended families.

Don't worry about skipping ahead, looking for the "blended family" subheading in these pages. I believe the principles I'm going to talk about here will definitely apply to everyone, no matter what parenting situation you're in.

I'm often fascinated at what gets the "likes" or the "hearts" or the "shares" or the re-tweets these days. Seriously – fascinated. I meant that. Most of what I see posted all over social media sites seems to me right out of the pages of Captain Obvious magazine. I mean, I don't want to sound condescending or anything, but I think you're all right there with me. I think what I'm learning about communication, now that everyone is doing it on a grander platform, is that the simpler stuff gains the most traction. Maybe the #1 rule in communication is true after all – KISS! (Keep it simple stupid) Ok, so I'm a slow learner. (Isn't this supposed to be written for a 3rd grader to read? Hope so, that's about all I got)

So, let me state the obvious. O wait, I already did – look up at the title of this chapter. Parent on the same page. Be a united front. Never undermine the discipline of your partner. Ever. In any way. Don't disagree with your spouse in front of the kids (ok, rarely, but if you do, do it with respect. A more effective way to disagree would be to back the co-parent in front of your kids, then take him/her aside privately to discuss your disagreement.) There – I said it. Didn't we learn that in parenting 101? Not so fast.

In reality, even if some of us have heard that somewhere before, most of us never saw that modeled, and as a matter of fact, we saw just the opposite! As
~~~~~

I stated back in chapter 1, if we haven't "dropped" our baggage, we not only run the risk of transferring it to our kids, but it can also rear it's ugly head when it comes to co-parenting. Couples have to work out their own stuff before they can be a team that can effectively tackle tough parenting situations.

Let me just give you a "hypothetical" scenario. Just for grins, I'll use the names "Brian" and "Jamie." (to protect the privacy of the actual couple in the example, you know the drill…)

Brian jumps his son for leaving the lights on in his room – AGAIN! (Backstory: In Brian's family growing up, kids were taught to turn off every light when leaving a room, and to make sure we don't go "in and out" of the house, or leave a door open for more than a few seconds, God forbid, because, after all, we weren't "air conditioning the entire city of Dallas!")

"Carson!" (we'll call the kid Carson for grins) "Carson! I just walked by your room and your lights were on and your fan was going full blast! I've told you a hundred times, turn off your lights when you're not in your room!

Now, Brian said that with a bit more volume and a harsher tone than Jamie would have voted for. In fact, in this case, as Jamie witnessed the scolding, she showed disapproval by giving Brian "the look" (the look an elementary school teacher gives a 2nd grader after she catches him doing something stupid, something "he knew better" than to do – you know, with the pursed lips and frowny eye brows?) Carson sees "the look" and sees my reaction to the look.

"What!? You don't agree? You think I'm being too hard on him? You don't recall me telling him 100 times?..."

(Backstory: In Jamie's family growing up, discipline was lacking in certain areas, especially compared to Brian's family. Brian recalls in his early visits to Jamie's family home, often they'd have every light on in every room, with every ceiling fan on high blast – you know – turning magazine pages on the coffee table full blast, with the front door propped wide open with the air conditioner running to beat the band. Brian remembers almost having a panic attack the first time he encountered this.)

So, as the scab gets ripped off the wound from some of the early humdinger fights between Brian and Jamie because of his perceived lack of discipline in Jamie due to her family of origin, he quickly gets agitated and defensive, and then goes on the offensive. As he begins to attack Jamie, throwing in the kitchen sink, she retreats into hurt, stonewalling mode, knowing the anal "hard-a$$ is on another rampage", and the best thing to do is just lay low.

Result? Carson receives several messages as he tries to process the confusing scene. I can almost hear his self-talk in those moments when he walks away unscathed, the attention turned away from him, and onto the parent's disagreement:

1. Hmm, looks like there's trouble in paradise.
2. Ah oh, dad's in trouble again!
3. No matter what happens with them, I'm certainly off the hook, that's for sure!
4. Man, I'm thankful mom was there to step in and get him off my back.
5. I wonder if dad's going to be even madder now?
6. Crud, I wonder what would happen if mom weren't here?
7. Did I cause that fight?
8. Hmm, I wonder if mom's going to blame that on me?
9. Maybe I should just turn my light off next time.

Even if I'm a horrible mind-reader, that was horrible parenting at it's best!

Ok, ok, so for those of you who didn't figure that out – that was US. Hypothetically, of course! We would never disagree over such a petty issue. Of course we would, and we did! It was years before we learned to reconcile our differences, forgive old resentments, and be a united front when it comes to disciplining our kids.

Parenting on the same page doesn't simply mean settling old scores between a Hatfield and a McCoy after they inter-marry. It's also learning to discuss disciplinary actions with your teammate before it's imposed or enforced. It's the pre-game meeting. In this meeting, you and your spouse talk about what action or behavior has led to the disciplinary action, and what corrective measures you are intending to impose, and for how long. Keeping in mind that your intended outcome is *correction* rather than *punishment* will guide you well.

In this meeting, both parents log in on what they think is appropriate, and one might even try to back one parent "off the ledge" if they believe they are intending to exact too harsh of a disciplinary action – the punishment doesn't fit the crime, so to speak. This is when you calm down, and allow logic and reason to override your initial emotional response to what your "fool kid" has done this time, and make sure you come up with a plan of action that you both feel comfortable with. The worst mistake you can make is going in half-cocked, or fully cocked, but with one parent "holding the gun," and the other parent feeling the need to "protect" the kid from the angry, out of control, emotional over-reactor.

I still remember the time I started reminding Christian that he was grounded and that he shouldn't be using his cell phone, and Jamie chimed in, "well, that was last week." Woah woah woah. "Uh, can I see you in the kitchen for a minute, baby?" What ensued was an unpleasant *post*-game meeting, after a loss – not nearly as effective as the *pre*-game meeting I was describing earlier. In another instance, (not too long after this one), I pulled Jamie into the bedroom (it's not what you think), and I said, "Ok, are you ok with me taking his keys and cell phone away for an entire month?" (I'll keep you in suspense as to Jamie's answer and what we ended up doing in that instance) The point is, that BEFORE sitting down with our son, and discussing the consequences of his repeated disobedience and lack of respect for his curfew, and a couple of other things, Jamie and I came to an agreement on how we were going to parent in that situation, so one didn't feel the need to back the truck up once we began discussing it with him. Ok, so I can't stand it – yes, we did take his cell phone and keys for 1 month. Yep, 1 month. I know you're thinking that's so extreme – and how inconvenient – for us! All that is true, and it's the best thing we ever did – worked amazingly well, and Christian never had his phone or keys taken again. Come on – he missed curfew 5 times in a row! (see chapter 4 about brain-dead 16 year old boys)

Chapter 6

Say You're Sorry

~~~~~

"As for parents, don't provoke your children to anger, but raise them with discipline and instruction about the Lord."
~~~~~

Ephesians 6:4[7]

Earlier, I talked about apologizing to my daughter when I realized I had jumped on her for doing exactly what I taught her to do – disrespecting her mother. Like I said, I think that apology went a long way. Here's the deal – our kids know we're not perfect. They know we screw up. They watch us do it in a variety of ways every day. None of us wants to admit that we're helping screw up our kids, but we are. It's an undeniable fact. We'll get some things right, but we get a lot of things wrong.

Just the other day, after a not so stellar example of loving, respectful communication with my wife, Carson, my 13 year old, said, "Dad, why do you do that?" I turned to him a bit frustrated because he was, of course, butting into something that was none of his business. I barked, "Why do I do what?" Then he said something that stung about as bad as anything I had heard in a while. He didn't hesitate, "Torment mom until she says what you want to hear." OUCH. (for a split second, prior to launching into my defense, trying to convince him that he didn't understand what we were talking about, that I was having trouble understanding her from the other room, and that he needed to mind his own business…prior to all that, I actually flashed back to the conversation with a couple in my office earlier this particular day, thinking about how I passionately pontificated the importance of modeling well for their children, blah, blah, BLAH, BARF!)

But, my mouth overrode my brain, and I began to try to talk my 8th grader out of what he had just witnessed. The look on his face said it all. He didn't speak, but his expression spoke volumes, "Dad, don't embarrass yourself any worse than you already have, and don't patronize me by actually thinking you can justify this behavior. I'm smarter than that."

That pesky voice that visits me from time to time tapped the familiar tap on my shoulder, pretty much cutting right to the chase. "Shut up." But… "Shhh."

So, I sat in silence for about a minute, thinking about what had just happened. He was absolutely right. Not the voice, although he's predictably and annoyingly spot on. That's a given. Carson was right. Busted. Kid catches dad screwing up again. Now what are you gonna do about it? I'd love to be able to tune into the thoughts that are swirling around right now in the collective heads of hundreds (or handful) of people that are reading this at the moment. Undoubtedly, we're all conjuring up the most recent similar scenario, or the one that we feel the most guilty about. So, what are you gonna do about it?

You see, that question isn't just part of the story, the rhetorical question I posed to myself after I was caught in the act! I'm asking *you* that. How do you respond when you know you've blown it, whether or not your kid actually has the courage to call you out on it? By the way, I so love that mine does/do! (twerp)

Even though the apostle Paul quotes it in his letter to the Ephesians, it's actually a proverb – "Parents, don't provoke your children to anger." You want to piss a kid off? Don't admit when you've blown it, then come down on them for their crap. That'll do it. They'll not only disrespect you, but they'll come up with all sorts of appropriate names for you, hypocrite being one of the more polite.

I know I left you in suspense – (someone told me to try to build some cliff hanging moments, so I hope you actually remember where I left you, and haven't nodded off). Following the lesson initiated by my middle-schooler, I knew I had to do 2 things. So, after that minute of silence, I first went to Jamie and said, "Baby, I'm sorry I treated you that way, and I'm sorry I took my frustration about the situation out on you." Then I came back, sat down and locked eyes with my way-too-smart for-his-own-good son, and said, "Hey, look at me. I'm sorry. I'm sorry, I talked to your mom that way." He kind of half grinned, saying, "It's ok." That was it. It's ok.

Rather than me telling you what went through his mind, and what that apology did for Carson, I wanted to include his own words. So, as I wrote this chapter, I asked him. Here's his reply:

"What I thought after you said you were sorry?"

"Um"

"I don't know."

So, there you have it. Hahahaha. I know you were wanting something more – TRUST ME – SO WAS I!! But that was it. Come on, he's an 8th grade boy!

Let me fill in some blanks for you though. My son and I are close. Really close. Here's what I know. Little walls get erected every day that will kill intimacy, and that destroy bonds between a father and a son, or a mother and a daughter. Through pride, those walls can be reinforced, built taller, and divide further. With humility, they can be torn down, not allowed to get in the way of a close, loving relationship. I believe apologies tear down walls.

It's so hard to say "I'm sorry," though, isn't it? Elton John seems to think so – wrote a hit song saying as much. Even Fonzie (yes, I'm really dating myself with a Happy Days reference) struggled to say I was "wrrrrrrr." I was "wrrrrr."

Damn pride. Gonna be the death of us all. Was for Satan. Bible says it comes before a fall. I mean, that's the deal. We all hate to admit we're wrong, and we're so afraid of taking <u>blame</u> – rhymes with **shame!**!! Isn't that it? Aren't we all afraid that somehow, whether God, or fellow man, or some judge or jury somewhere, someone is going to vote us off the island? We're gonna be sent packing, or some trap door is going to open and we're going straight to hell, without passing GO, or collecting $200?

For whatever reason, saying I'm sorry is a bitch, for sure, but it's one of the most important things you'll ever learn to do as a parent (and a spouse.) When I do family mediations, helping facilitate conversations between parents and kids, I see why it's so hard to apologize. The resentment has built through the years, and the teenager is now trying to explain why they are acting out in this way or that. The parent hears the child describe specific instances where they felt abandoned, favored "less than" a sibling, unduly punished or what have you, and the scathing critique cuts the parent to the quick. Our first impulse as parents is to be defensive – I mean, we're under attack! How dare our snot-nosed kid tell us how the cow ate the cabbage. "Let me tell *you* something, mister!..." We want to lay into them, giving them our recollection of the events, our side of the story. In doing this, many times we unknowingly invalidate the feelings of our children, making them feel that their voice isn't heard, or simply doesn't matter. Are kids always right? Of course not. Do they deserve to be heard, though. Absolutely.

I remember when my dad and I were hashing through some old stuff that I had carried around for years, and that I was finally working through and letting go. I felt I had to let him know that I had forgiven he and mom for some things that had hurt my feelings years earlier. Naturally, he saw the events and circumstances differently than I did, and again, naturally, was defensive. I was simply trying to help him understand how I had been hurt, but he was hearing me criticize him. At one point in the conversation, he said

“I’m sorry, Brian…” and I interrupted him, and said, “Dad, I don’t need an apology. I’ve already forgiven you.” Now perplexed I think, my dad then said, “Then what do you want from me?” I said, “ I want a relationship with you.” There it was. That’s what my heart was seeking, not just to understand or to be understood. I wanted a relationship with my father that had suffered in my early adulthood due to resentments that had built, due mostly from lack of communication, and due to pride on both of our parts.

Something changed that day. I knew my dad wasn’t interested in “being right” or telling me what I was supposed to think or feel. He sought to listen that day, and as he did, I found myself more willing to listen to him, hearing things from him that gave me insight into those situations that I hadn’t understood before. As I heard his words, I’m sorry, I knew in my heart that forgiveness was done, and that a wall was being torn down that day. And although a bit geographically estranged, I love my dad more than he knows, and appreciate all he has done for me, all that he has taught me, and feel that our relationship is as good now as ever.

The story I’m about to relay could have well been told in Chapter 1, (handing off our baggage) but was saved until now to reiterate the importance of apologizing when we’ve blown it, but also reinforcing the point that we all HAVE and WILL blow it.

When Chandler was around 8 or 9 years old, Jamie and I were in the car on the way home from something, and Chan was in the back seat. Jamie and I began arguing and it escalated to the point where I was screaming at Jamie. As she gave me the big eyes, indicating that we shouldn’t be “doing this” in front of Chandler, I totally ignored her, and continued my verbal assault, even saying something to the effect that “I don’t care who hears,” and that “maybe she *needs* to hear this!” I was in a fit of rage, totally out of control, and I wasn’t going to be stopped.

When we finally pulled into the driveway, Chandler burst into tears, jumped out of the car, and ran inside, quickly up the stairs, and into her bathroom. Fuming, but almost “waking up” from my anger-induced episode, I noticed Chandler’s actions and went upstairs to check on her. As I came to the top of the stairs, and neared her bathroom, I heard the unmistakable sound of Chan throwing up. I was devastated.

It’s actually hard to put into words what I felt in that moment, and to be completely honest, it’s hard recalling this, typing the words, and not going back to the place of emptiness and shame that I felt in that moment.

What Chandler was feeling was undoubtedly what Jamie had felt numerous times up to that point in our marriage. So, there it was. I was hurting the two most important women in my life (yes, Chan now 8 would certainly carry some of this into her adulthood). Hurt seems way too light of a word. Damage, destruction, carnage – these are more appropriate. As I sat with my back to the bathroom door, head in hands, I began to weep and I mustered one thought – "Lord, heal me, or kill me, but I never want to hurt these women like this again."

Around this same time, Jamie and I were again in an argument in the car (seems to be a favorite place to start crap – when you have a captive audience) and as she got more and more worked up, (I realized I was getting under her skin) I smugly turned to her and with a smirk made an extremely disrespectful comment. (I would actually tell you what it was, but I honestly don't remember) What I do recall is that Jamie began to hit me in my arm, over and over, blow after blow, as she began to sob. Now hear this loudly and clearly, Jamie had never before, and hasn't since, ever hit me. Ever. And as her fist landed repeatedly into my right shoulder, I literally pulled the car over fearing losing control of the vehicle. Jamie finally wore herself out, and sat sobbing in my front seat. As we sat at the side of the road off of 377, I had no inclination, not the slightest impulse to hit back in that moment. Again, the feeling was utter shame and emptiness. The voice again surfaced, and said "Look what you created. You did this." While I'm very careful not to give the idea that we can "make" people do things – yes, everyone is responsible for their REactions – I truly know in my heart, this wasn't who Jamie was, and isn't who she is. She was truly pushed to this – or better said, was "formed" into this by years of verbal and emotional abuse. She had simply had enough.

So…did I apologize? Of course. As we ragers know, once the bomb blows up, the PSI is now again in a manageable place – until the next time. So, yes, I apologized – I felt HORRIBLE about what had taken place, as I always did after I exploded, making a fool of myself, and hurting people that I loved. I had to do more than apologize. There couldn't be a next time. Actions speak louder than words, and I knew I had to BE different. I needed transformation. I needed help. Admitting this to ourselves is the first step toward change and healing. Blaming others, regardless if they carried some fault or not, and justifying our behavior in any way, will never lead to healing. There is no justification for fits of rage or destructive anger. It is never ok. Never.

This began a new journey (yes, even after marriage counseling and significant healing in certain areas) for me of seeking help and deeper understanding of myself, my past wounds, and where the deep-seeded anger truly came from. I thank God, that healing came, and that I became the man that I was created to be. Not a perfect man, not even close, but a man who doesn't lead his wife to hit him, and doesn't cause his daughter to throw up.

So, for many of us, the next step toward healing our relationships that have been strained or broken is seeking help, and committing to the steps that lead to change, not simply saying we're sorry. Parents, listen to me. It's not too late. As long as you have breath, it's not too late. As long as your son or daughter is still breathing, it's not too late. Seek help, and do the steps necessary to process and heal the issues that lead to your anger, or your brokenness. (again, see Appendix for resources)

Chapter 7
Love is Spelled T-I-M-E

~~~~~

" When you coming home son, I don't know when
We'll get together then, you know we'll have a good time then.. "

Harry Chapin[8]

Depending on how old you are, how old your kids are, and how "well" you deem yourself to be doing in this area, this chapter has the potential to be one of the most haunting, regretful chapters, or make you feel worthy of the "Parent of the Month" parking space at the Hall of Amazing Parents Museum. Simple reason: when time is gone, it's gone. We don't get it back. We all have a finite, allotted amount of time for our lives, and we either spend it wisely, or we waste it. We hate to put it in these absolute terms, don't we? Can't we kind of grade on the curve? I mean, "I don't waste ALL my time," or "yeah, I could probably have spent a *little* less time playing on-line poker last night." But, in any given moment, right now, you
~~~~~

are either using your time wisely, or wasting it. That's not to say that we have to be "working" or "productive" or other such over-achieving sounding words at any given moment. In some cases, recreation, or sleep is exactly what you *need* to be doing, and would be considered using your time wisely. Just a few months before my mom passed away, I asked her if she had it to do over, what would she change. Without batting an eye, she answered, "I wouldn't have taken everything so seriously." There is an element of time in this statement of regret.

Time matters. Being intentional about how we use our time matters. Really matters. When it comes to raising our kids, it is paramount. Let's all say it together – "They grow up so quickly" "It seems like just yesterday…" "Where has all the time gone?" Earlier this year, Jamie and I pulled onto 540 South in Fayetteville, and sat quietly for the next 10 or so miles before I finally broke the silence. Prior to this, I literally couldn't speak due to the HOG sized lump in my throat. We had just dropped off our son, Christian, at the University of Arkansas for his Freshman year. When I finally dared to defile the sacred, heavy air that hung in the front seat between my wife and me, I mustered (lip and voice quivering), "It literally feels like yesterday we were driving away from dropping him off at Kindergarten, watching him walk away from us, into his classroom, wondering if he was ready for the world." Jamie didn't speak for another 10 miles.

Nothing tells our kids we love them more than spending time with them. I'm kind of tired of the Q word when it comes to time. Sometimes "quality" time is simply used to justify "not enough" time. Uninterrupted, undistracted, long periods of time spent with our kids sends the message "you're worth it for me to be here." You're worth it. You are worth more than my friend's post on Instagram. You are worth more than my favorite TV show (that's recorded so I can watch it any time I want!) You are worth more than Ellen's latest tweet, or surfing Facebook. You are worth more than this email, my work, our finances, and the other 50 things I spend time on every day. Notice I didn't say *waste* time on everyday. We have to work, we have to spend time relaxing, and I'm a huge fan of having a variety of hobbies, interests, and activities to passionately pursue. We just have to keep them in perspective, and properly prioritize them *beneath* our families. If you're too busy for your kids, for whatever reason, not only might they believe that you care about *that thing* more than you care about them, but they also may subtly get the message that they aren't that significant – not just to you, but to anyone. In other words, this could initiate or reinforce the lie that attacks their identity, and makes them believe that they just don't matter much as a person. You show me a kid with a ton of confidence (I don't mean cockiness), and I'll show you a parent who has spent a lot of time hanging out with that kid, investing in their lives.

We first have to realize the HUGE impact the amount of time we spend with our kids truly has on them. Again, it really matters! Let me preface my next point with the fact that my father spent a lot of time with me. I have fond memories of dad playing "all time QB" with my brother and me, and how it felt when he'd zip our green nerf football with the little chunk out of the foam laces, right into my chest for a TD. I also remember his wheezy laugh as he stood, pre-dinner, in his work slacks with loosened tie after a hard day, watching me "chance it" in a b-ball game of around the world, knowing I'd go back to the start after bricking one off the front rim.

Dad was and is a good dad.

As I mentioned in Chapter 1, I was first introduced to the concept of "father wounds" reading a book by John Eldredge called Wild at Heart.[9] This book just illuminated feelings that many young men have as he articulates what all we need from our fathers that they simply weren't equipped to give. And when he talks about this, he's not just talking about the last generation, or generations gone by. He's talking about *every* generation. Bottom line, none of us receives all we need from our imperfect earthly fathers. (To help fill in the voids, I highly recommend Eldredge's sequel, Fathered By God) But that's not my primary point here. Where I'm going is, in reading Eldredge's book, I was struck with just how important it is to be intentional, wide awake, and fully alert to the fact that every interaction with our kids matter, and TIME is a huge factor in helping the next generation feel loved, and equipped to love and parent their children well. When you're acutely aware of this, and your son walks up to you and says, "Hey dad, wanna go throw the football?", you think twice before saying, "Not now, son, I'm busy," or "Not now, son, I'm tired." Ah, the dreaded words of the 13 year old – busy, tired, not today, not right now, maybe later.

Knowing that every moment is creating moment*um* in a certain direction makes it easier to make a wise decision when answering your child's bid for connection. I've shared this insight with my boys in several "teachable moments" trying to not only model what I've learned, but also trying to let them in on the concepts, so that they're already connecting the dots, learning to be intentional in their valued relationships. One day, after an extremely emotionally taxing day, Carson came to me the second I walked through the door (he sometimes runs out, and starts in on me as my car door swings open) and said, "Hey dad, change your clothes and let's play some basketball." I said, "Son, give me a minute, and I don't really feel like it tonight." Mind you, I coached my son's 4th, 5th, and 6th grade basketball teams, and during these years, we literally spent countless hours playing one on one in the driveway. These, not the games, were actually the valuable, precious, memory-building times in my book. A bit too smart for his own good, Carson quipped, "Come on dad, you're going to give me father wounds!"

That little shit. (sorry – haha)

It worked though. Damn guilt. (haha – sorry again)

Almost every night, Carson nods on his way up to bed, and says, "Come on." Yes, we still tuck him in. (Now, quickly, before my son is mortified, I have to tell you this isn't story time, with pacifier and feety pajamas. Carson has always enjoyed one on one time with both me and Jamie, separately, before he goes to bed. We spend it doing all sorts of relaxing bed-time rituals that spoil him to death. When he began protesting about me "tucking him in" at a too cool for school age, I protested right back with, "Hey, a son is never too old to be tucked in." To this day, it worked. Shh!) Now back to his nightly request. Recently, Carson, on his way up has said, "Mom, can you tuck me in?" On these increasingly frequent occasions, where he asks for mom only, I say, "Hey! What about me? Am I chopped liver?" To which he quickly says, "I knew you wouldn't come, you're always playing poker or chess."

Ouch!

Some of those times, I WAS really working. Well, a couple. (cough cough)

So, are there times when work HAS to be done. Absolutely. The Bible says "if a man doesn't work, neither shall he eat." (Neither shall his wife or kids. Somebody has to pay for the basketball uniforms.) Are there times when you need time for yourself, your spouse, your hobbies, recreation, sleep, etc.? Absolutely. There needs to be a healthy balance of all those things in your life, and if you're intentional about decision-making regarding your time, and have your kids in their proper place on your priority list, then you'll make wiser decisions which in turn will instill in your kids a sense of value, worth, and love that will solidify their identity, helping them more than a hundred

"Bible lessons." (no offense christians, remember I work for a church)

In our society, just the way the world works, does create a bit of a conundrum when it comes to balancing work and family life. I mean, you have to work to eat. I get that. And while you might have your priorities in the proper order, your employer may not share that value system. If you won't work those 70 hours a week, we'll find someone who will. Sure, that's a possibility, and a reality for some of you. Couple of things here. One, what's a job worth? Is it worth losing your family, or a good relationship with your son or daughter? Truly. You need to evaluate that. Two, many times, even if we work long hours, and have a demanding employer, and switching jobs or industries simply isn't a viable option, and might even be a stupid financial decision for our families, many of us still have some disposable, and even "quality" time left over for our families/kids. It's just that THAT time, too, gets wasted or robbed.

It's sad when you think about it. Someone has their priorities in place – they want to be a good parent, desire to spend time with their kids, but then when they get home from a long day, something happens. Tonight was going to be different. You had great intentions! But you are…wait for it…TIRED!

I know I've already mentioned being tired as a reason we don't spend time with our kids, but I wanted to hit it again, because it's so common. It's universal. We are all tired. Try this – ask someone today, "How's it going?" Edging out "fine" for the most popular response these days – "I'm tired!" Ok, I get it. Trust me, I'm one of the most sleep deprived men on the planet. But I also get ribbed by my close friends about being one of the highest energy guys they know (not just for my age). So, what's the secret? What's my secret? What's the secret to having enough energy to spend time with your kids? I could start preaching here about a lot of things I truly believe in, or things I do. For example, I understand that most of us eat like crap most of the time, and the food we eat makes us lethargic. I could talk about how drinking green smoothies full of spinach and kale and other stuff that most humans have no desire to consume on a regular basis can make us healthier and give us more energy. But I won't talk about that. I could also talk about drinking energy drinks in the afternoon when you know you're going to be asked in the driveway to pitch to your son, or ride ripsticks or go fishing. There are actually semi-healthy energy drinks. But I won't talk about that. I could talk about getting more sleep, since you're not being a good steward of your physical body due to sleep deprivation, killing your energy – but I won't talk about that (mostly because it'd be hypocritical).

Here's what I will say. Do whatever it takes! Do what works for you! Do whatever you have to do! It matters. It really matters, so do whatever it is that reminds you of the importance passionately pursuing time with your kids, and fuel that passion the best way you can.

One final note about this. Pay close attention to what it is your kid actually *wants* to do when spending time with you. I could say that it doesn't matter WHAT you actually do – just spending time with you is what they want. And that is definitely true to a degree. But many times, parents selfishly arrange times with their kids doing things that the parent wants to do, rather than considering getting involved with the kids on their turf, doing things that the kid is interested in. That's better than nothing, but you want to watch a kid light up, feel significant, and loved? Then get involved with activities/hobbies/interests/sports/music/games that *they* love. I hate when I catch my son, Carson, looking back towards my face when he's showing me his latest drawing, or Instagram edit, or game. I realize he's having to check every few seconds if he still actually has my attention, or if I've already turned back to my phone. I hate that. But I'm guilty. Put down the damn phone, Brian. It can wait. Carson is 13. He's in 8th grade. But trust me, I'm going to blink, and I'll be getting onto 540 South in Fayetteville…

So, the next time you sign a card for your kid, make sure you can sign it:

Time,

dad

www.ingramcontent.com/pod-product-compliance
Lightning Source LLC
LaVergne TN
LVHW040931150826
845672LV00007B/2297

* 9 7 9 8 5 0 4 7 9 1 1 5 9 *